Explore the Aztec Empire

Candice Ransom

Lerner Publications ◆ Minneapolis

Lerner Publications Company
An imprint of Lerner Publishing Group, Inc.
241 First Avenue North
Minneapolis, MN 55401 USA

For reading levels and more information, look up this title at www.lernerbooks.com.

Main body text set in Billy Infant Regular. Typeface provided by SparkyType.

Editor: Angel Kidd **Photo Editor:** Angel Kidd
Lerner team: Sue Marquis

Library of Congress Cataloging-in-Publication Data

Names: Ransom, Candice F., 1952- author
Title: Explore the Aztec Empire / Candice Ransom.
Description: Minneapolis, MN : Lerner Publications, [2026] | Series: Lightning bolt books - early civilizations | Includes bibliographical references and index. | Audience: Ages 6-9 | Audience: Grades 2-3 | Summary: "The Aztecs built an empire on two swampy islands in Lake Texcoco. They thrived until Spanish explorers came and took control. From farming to warfare, readers will learn about the daily life of the Aztecs"— Provided by publisher.
Identifiers: LCCN 2025013533 (print) | LCCN 2025013534 (ebook) | ISBN 9798765689301 library binding | ISBN 9798348028992 paperback | ISBN 9798765696903 epub
Subjects: LCSH: Aztecs—Juvenile literature | Mexico—Civilization—Juvenile literature | Mexico—History—To 1519—Juvenile literature
Classification: LCC F1219.73 .R365 2026 (print) | LCC F1219.73 (ebook) | DDC 972/.018—dc23/eng/20250606

LC record available at https://lccn.loc.gov/2025013533
LC ebook record available at https://lccn.loc.gov/2025013534

Manufactured in the United States of America
1-1012507-54798-6/4/2025

Table of Contents

From Island to Empire

The Aztec people lived about seven hundred years ago. They created a large civilization. A civilization is a group of people who live in an area and form a community.

The Aztecs were farmers and warriors. They wandered for years looking for a place to settle. In 1325, they chose two swampy islands in the middle of Lake Texcoco.

The Aztecs believed they had to build their city where they saw an eagle eating a snake.

They knew it would not be easy to build a city on a swamp. But they worked together to figure out how.

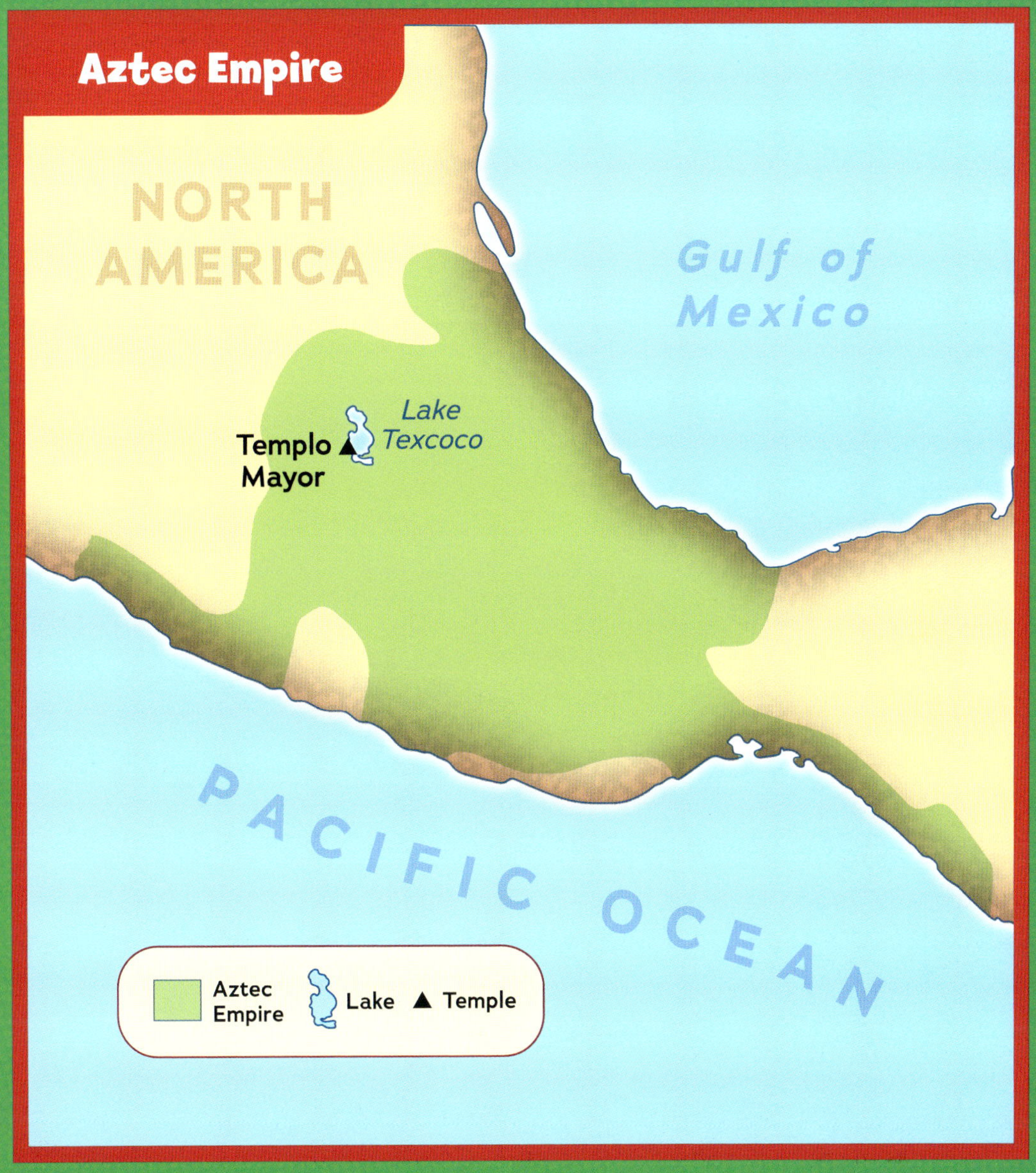

Lake Texcoco was in the Valley of Mexico. The valley had five lakes and was surrounded by volcanoes and mountains.

Aztec kings created an empire by taking other people's lands. **An empire is a large area where people are ruled by one person.**

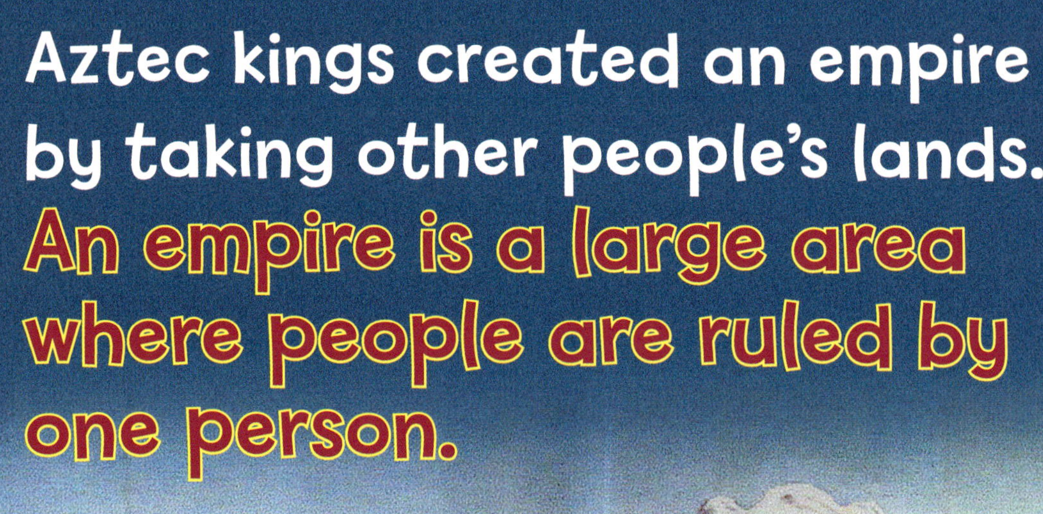

This painting shows the Aztec city in 1519.

A Civilization Is Created

Aztec workers built raised roads across Lake Texcoco. They carried logs and stones from the mainland to their island. They dug canals and built canoes to travel through the valley.

Their first houses were made of clay and wood. Markets were built along wide streets to trade and sell goods. Some people crafted pottery or gold jewelry.

Snakes were important to the Aztecs.

Many people from the mainland moved to the great island city. Itzcóatl was the fourth king of the Aztecs and the founder of their empire.

The king joined with other civilizations to bring more people into the empire. The new citizens farmed or built buildings.

Kings ruled the empire for many years.

The Aztecs were skilled farmers.

Aztec women wove cotton into cloth. Men practiced fighting. Girls learned to cook and weave. Boys hunted ducks and fished. Everyone had a job.

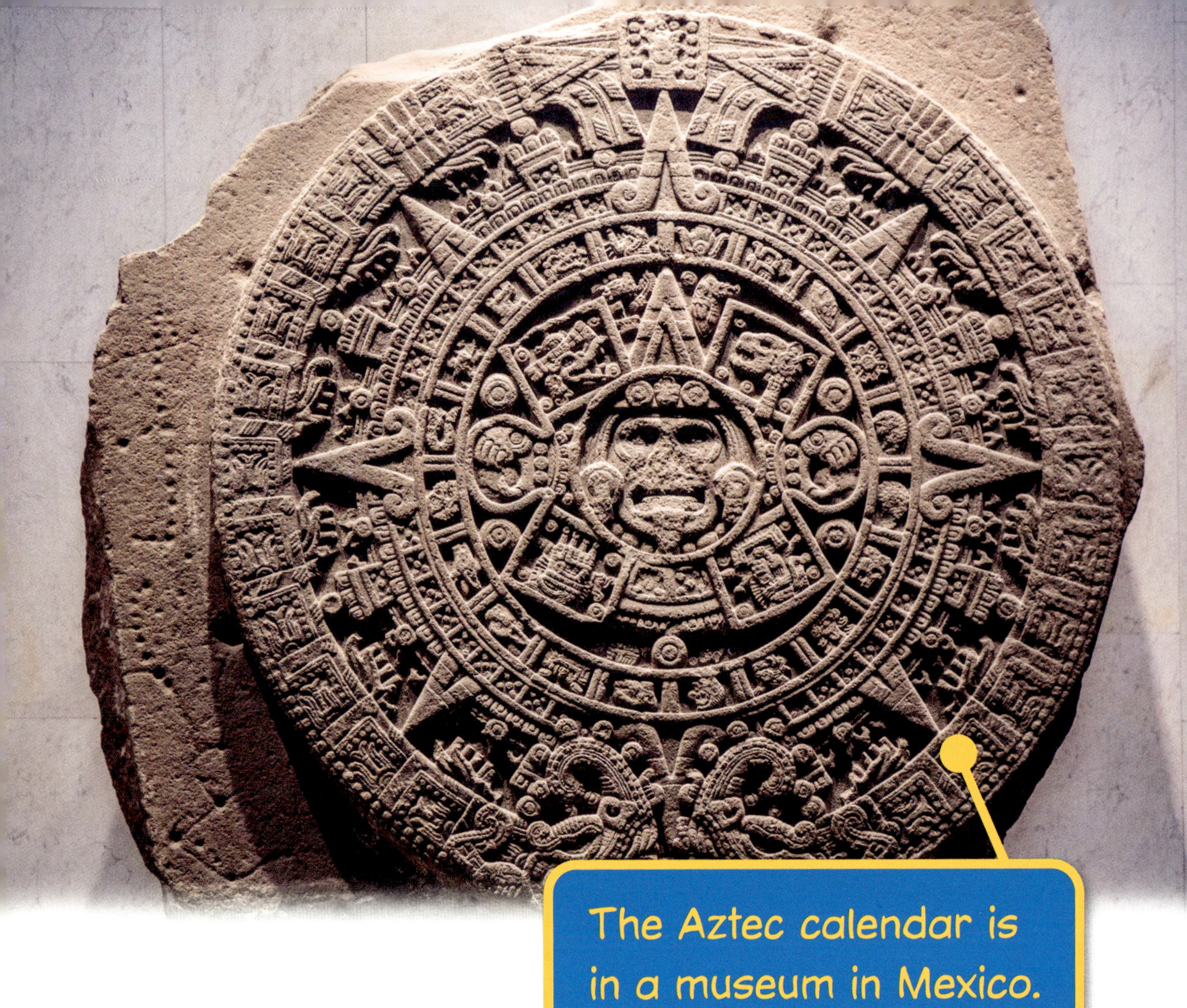

The Aztec calendar is in a museum in Mexico.

The Aztec year was guided by two calendars carved on a piece of lava rock. The round stone was 12 feet (3.7 m) across. **Their sun god was engraved in the center.**

Priests performed ceremonies to honor the Aztec gods of war and rain at the Templo Mayor. The huge stone temple rose 197 feet (60 m) into the sky.

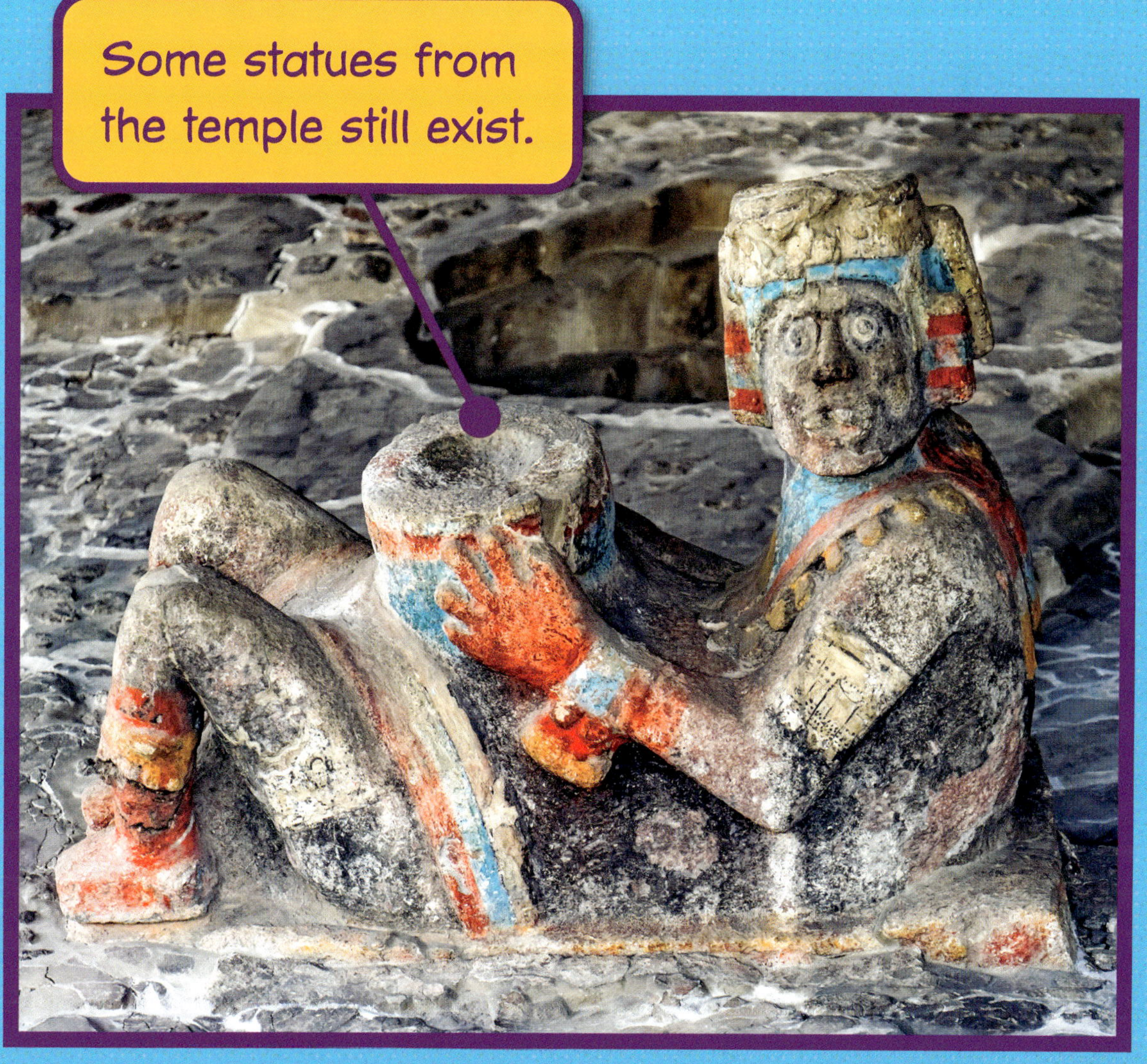

Some statues from the temple still exist.

Strangers Arrive

In 1519, eleven ships landed in what we now call Mexico. Spanish explorer Hernán Cortés brought five hundred soldiers, one hundred sailors, and sixteen horses to the Aztec Empire.

Some Native peoples helped the Spanish build and fight.

Cortés wanted new land for Spain. Thousands of Native people joined his Spanish army in his war against the Aztecs.

Cortés fought the Aztecs in their own island city and won. **By 1521, the Aztec civilization was gone.** Cortés's people built a new city in place of the Aztec capital.

Cortés called it Mexico City, claiming the country of Mexico for Spain. Today, people have discovered ancient Aztec ruins beneath the modern streets of Mexico City.

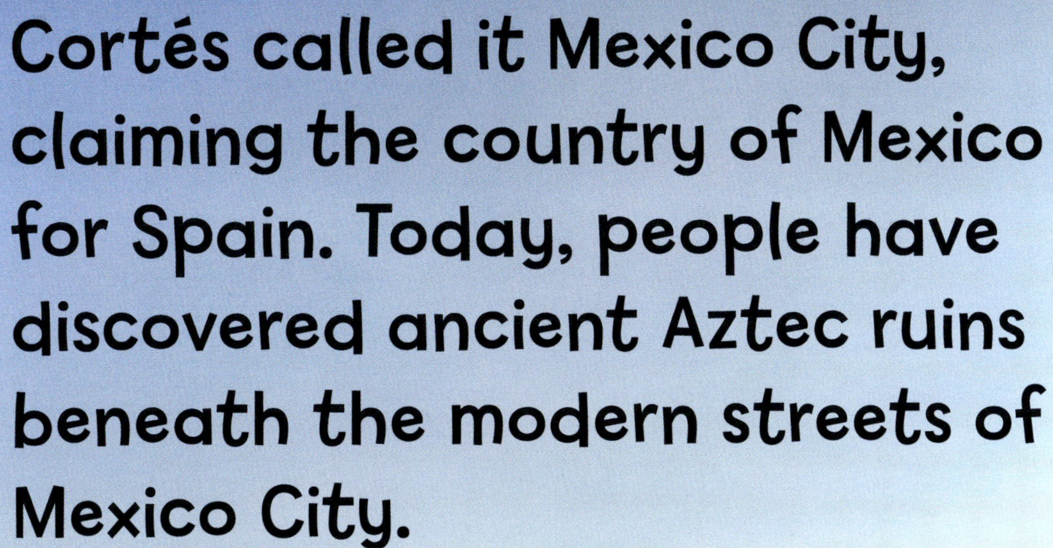

A Look at Floating Farms

The Aztecs invented a way to grow crops on Lake Texcoco. They hammered wooden stakes into the lake bottom to hold woven mats. Soil was piled on the mats, and seeds were planted on them. Hundreds of floating gardens grew corn, beans, squash, tomatoes, and other vegetables. Instead of one harvest season, the Aztecs had seven each year.

Aztec Empire Facts

- A legend said the Aztec people would settle in the place where they saw an eagle on a cactus eating a snake. That symbol is on Mexico's flag.
- The Aztecs were shocked to see Cortés riding a horse. They had never seen horses before.
- The Aztecs were the first to celebrate the Day of the Dead. People of Mexican heritage still celebrate it from November 1 to November 2.

Glossary

ancient: very old

canal: a human-made waterway for boats or for watering plants

ceremony: a formal act or series of acts performed in a certain way

civilization: a large group of people who live in an area and share a common government and culture

community: a group of people who live close together or have shared interests

lava: melted rock from a volcano

Native: the people who originally lived in a place

priest: a religious leader who performs ceremonies

Learn More

Andrews, Elizabeth. *The Aztecs*. DiscoverRoo, 2023.

Britannica Kids: Aztec
https://kids.britannica.com/kids/article/Aztec/352810

History for Kids: Aztecs
https://historyforkids.org/category/aztecs

National Geographic Kids: Aztec Civilization
https://kids.nationalgeographic.com/history/article/aztec-civilization

O'Neill, Sean. *50 Things You Didn't Know About Mexico*. Red Chair, 2025.

Orozco, Polo. *Day of the Dead: A Celebration of Life*. Golden Books, 2024.

Index

Photo Acknowledgments

Image credits: ART Collection/Alamy, p. 4; DEA/G. DAGLI ORTI/Getty Images, p. 5; SamuelSPMX/Shutterstock, p. 6; Laura Westlund/Independent Picture Service, p. 7; IanDagnall Computing/Alamy, p. 8; Nicholas Gill/Alamy, pp. 9, 20; mauritius images GmbH/Alamy, p. 10; mikroman6/Getty Images, p. 11; Niday Picture Library/Alamy, p. 12; Art Collection 2/Alamy, p. 13; Jos Antonio Crdenas Zetina/500px/Getty Images, p. 14; bpperry/Getty Images, p. 15; THEPALMER/Getty Images, p. 16; PRISMA ARCHIVO/Alamy, p. 17; KenWiedemann/Getty Images, p. 18; Sergio Mendoza Hochmann/Getty Images, p. 19.

Cover: Robert Peddle/500px/Getty Images.